The Gardener's PLANNER

---- **&** ----

LOGBOOK

a 5-year record and tracker of *your garden*

chartwell
books

THIS BOOK BELONGS TO

_____

Contents

Introduction

A garden is what you make of it: Potted plants on a patio. A slender patch of tulips along a walkway. Raised beds for a variety of vegetables. A coveted spot at the community garden. Whether this is your first foray into gardening, or you're a perennial green thumb, this book has something for you.

As more than a garden planner and logbook, the thoughtful prompts and expert tips in these pages will help you develop a garden that's more personal and ultimately more rewarding. Start by thinking about what you want to plant, focusing on your garden goals while setting realistic expectations. Then get your hands dirty when you start to plant, maintain, and tend to your garden. Finally, you'll get to celebrate your wonderful harvest in the fall and record your triumphs (and tragedies).

While much of this book focuses on edible gardening, it does not overlook the fact that flowers and perennial plants are a part of many gardens. The advice, tips, and log pages here will apply to any garden you've set your mind to. Let's get started.

A Garden Primer

No matter where you live, winter and early spring is typically a time for garden dormancy. It's also a time for planning and for dreaming. What kind of garden do you really want—and is this the year you're going to make it happen? Or, what kind of garden do you think you can actually manage? Are you looking for showy foliage, flowers to cut, vegetables to harvest, or perennial fruit bushes? Care-free and low-maintenance? Shady or sunny? Use the pages that follow to plan your dream garden—or your realistic adventures—from the ground up. As the days start to lengthen, you'll start putting all that planning into practice.

GETTING TO THE ROOT OF THINGS

There are as many reasons for planting a garden as there are gardeners. Think about what having a garden means to you. Is it for how it looks, or is it for the tangibles it provides (flowers, vegetables, herbs)—or both? Did you have a garden growing up, or did you never have space for a garden, and you've always wanted one? Are you looking for stress relief and a bit of exercise? Think about your garden goals.

TAKE A WALK

How can you become inspired to plant your garden if you don't look at your surroundings? Get outside! Notice how the light falls, even though it will change throughout the growing season. Imagine where you might want to expand your garden size, create a walking path, or add a trellis. Take note of large trees or bushes that might cast shade. (Remember that while most vegetables and herbs require at least six hours of direct sunlight daily, fall-weather crops that start out in the summer might appreciate that shade.)

Take accurate measurements of your garden space. Write them here:

_____

_____

_____

_____

_____

DOWN TO EARTH

Now think about the reality of what your garden can actually be, using the space you have. Are there any obstacles you face, or is your space ready to grow? For example, if your house is on a hill or your yard is more slate than soil, do you need to build raised beds or buy several containers? Or, if you have a large backyard, do you need to till the ground where you want the row garden to be? Will there be challenges to watering your garden where you want it, or will you need to fence it in to protect it from wildlife?

_____

_____

_____

_____

_____

BEGINNER TOOLS AND CROPS

Gardening with the proper tools will make the whole experience much more enjoyable, but you needn't break the bank buying every gizmo imaginable. Buy the best you can afford and give full-size tools a test drive: see how the handle feels in your hands, whether the height is right for you, if it's too heavy, etc. Below is a basic tools list, depending on your garden needs. As you progress, you might find you'll want to add a few more items, such as a wheelbarrow, kneeling pad, garden gloves, buckets, etc.

Spade or shovel		
Digging fork or hoe		
Garden rake		
Trowel		
Pocketknife or pruning shears		
Hose or watering can		

RULE OF (GREEN) THUMB: To help your tools last longer, store them in a dry place, and don't put them away dirty.

If this is your first foray into gardening, go easy on yourself. Start small, buy transplants, and opt for easy plants that are sure to reward your efforts, such as most herbs; cucumbers, green beans, lettuce, strawberries, summer squash, tomatoes; and alyssum, hostas, impatiens, marigolds, phlox, sunflowers, and zinnias. Ask for tips at your local garden supply store or nursery.

Remember that gardens are full of life—and like life, they don't always go as planned. Be prepared for some things to not thrive, but also try to have some fun. Plant something you've never tried before, like peanuts or okra or rhubarb. If they don't grow well, that's okay! And if they do (and you don't like them), there's *always* someone who's willing to take fresh-grown produce off your hands.

PLANNING FOR PESTS AND FINDING FRIENDS

While it's tempting to design a garden according to aesthetics alone, it's important to keep in mind that some plants will draw unwanted attention, in the form of insects, to other plants.

Luckily, there are plenty of plants that attract bugs to snack on the pesky interlopers. These friends, or beneficials, come in all shapes and sizes. **Pollinators**, such as butterflies and bumblebees, help your plants grow and produce fruit. **Predators**, such as praying mantis and ladybugs, will eat other insects. Then there's the *Alien* version where the **parasitizer** insect lays eggs in or on other insects, leaving a midnight snack for the larvae when they hatch. The best way to attract beneficials is by offering them food—which would be flower nectar and pollen before the pests start to flourish—and by *not* spraying insecticides.

Don't forget about two- and four-legged predators! Depending on where you live, your local wildlife will all want to have a crack at your garden buffet. What daytime dwellers and nighttime callers do you have lurking in your yard? Clues include holes (burrows) in your garden soil or yard, animal tracks and droppings, and damage to existing plants.

Keep in mind that most pests are highly motivated, and deterrence can be difficult. Some things that might help keep them out include chicken wire, fencing, bird netting, nontoxic and biodegradable repellents, motion lights, planting in tall containers, and adding deterrent plants.

SEEDS VS. SEEDLINGS

As with most things garden related, your climate zone will dictate what you can plant and when. If your growing season is short, it makes sense to start your garden with plants rather than seeds. However, buying seed packets is more economical than buying packs of seedlings. For this reason, many people like to get a jump on the growing season by starting their plants indoors as seeds.

There are many ways to start seeds, but pay attention to whether the seeds are direct seeding (or direct sowing). This means that the seeds do better if planted directly in the garden rather than transplanted as seedlings. Seedlings that you buy, on the other hand, are great for plants that take a long time to bear fruit and in climates with late or early frosts. You can find a lot of information on your seed packets, including:

- optimal planting zone;
- days to maturity;
- when to sow relative to your first and last frost dates;
- and, in some cases, when seeds should be started indoors.

The USDA has a Plant Hardiness Zone Map that many gardeners use to determine which plants will thrive in their yards. Zones are based on the average annual winter temperatures, with 1 being the coldest and 10 the warmest. To find your zone, check the map on the back of a seed packet or look online for an interactive map or hardiness zone converter where you can enter your zip code. Write your zone here.

_____

COOL-WEATHER PLANTS FOR TRANSPLANTING

Broccoli

Brussels sprouts

Cabbage

Cauliflower

Lettuce

Kohlrabi

COOL-WEATHER PLANTS FOR DIRECT SOWING

Beans

Beets

Mustards

Parsnips

Peas

Radishes

Turnips

Spinach

STARTING SEEDS INDOORS

Depending on your climate (and budget), you might want to start growing seeds indoors. When to start really depends on which seeds, how long they take to germinate, and when your last frost is. For the seeds you want to start indoors, there's no time like the winding down of winter to begin.

Here's what you'll need:

- Seeds
- Seed-starting mix
- Clean containers 2½ inches to 3 inches (about 7 cm) tall
- Waterproof tray to put the containers on (optional)
- Labels

Here's what you'll do:

1. Fill the container with mix, tap it to settle the dirt, and moisten it.

2. Follow the directions on the seed packet for how deep to plant the seeds. (Don't plant too many in one container since you'll have to thin them before you can even transplant them.)

3. If space permits, plant the seeds in multiple containers—more than you think you'll want as actual plants. You can choose the healthiest ones for transplanting later or, if they're all strong, share them with friends. (Most unused seeds will keep in a cool dry place for 3 to 5 years.)

Forcing bulbs is different than starting seeds. Your best source for how to do this is through a university's horticulture extension; there are many online with step-by-step instructions.

4. Don't forget to label your seeds!

5. To water, use a gentle mist from above, or set the containers in a tray or shallow pan with water in it; they'll absorb water over a few hours.

6. Put the seeds in a warm spot, such as near a television, on top of a refrigerator or water heater, or even near (but not on) a radiator.

7. As soon as the seedlings break through the soil, move them to a sunny location—a south-facing window is perfect—and rotate them every day so stems don't develop a bend.

Containers can be mini pots that you buy at a garden center, but they can also be upcycled household items such as milk cartons, yogurt containers, ice cream pints, or egg cartons. (Be sure to punch a drainage hole in the bottom of anything plastic.) You might consider using biodegradable containers, such as peat pots, that can be planted right in the garden; one option with a twist: a plain ice cream cone (the flat-bottom kind).

CARING FOR TRANSPLANTS

While it's fairly easy to get a seed to germinate, the hard part comes in nurturing those seedlings into plants that are mature enough to be planted outdoors.

Keep the soil moist, and continue to rotate the plants in their sunny location. Humidity is also a seedling's friend, so if possible, plug in a humidifier nearby, or put them on your bathroom floor while you shower.

As the plants grow, you'll have to thin the crop. Overcrowding can impede your plants' growth. Pull out or snip off the smallest, most straggly seedings and discard. If you're reluctant to pull your seedlings, choose the hardiest-looking ones for transplanting to another container, leaving the stragglers behind. You know they're ready when they've developed two sets of true leaves.

Here's what you'll need:

- Containers (about 3 inches [7.5 cm] in diameter)
- Potting-soil mix
- Labels

Cole crops are cool-weather plants that can be planted in the spring—but they can also be planted later in the summer for a fall harvest. If you provide enough shade, you can often grow cool-weather crops such as spinach, peas, and lettuce throughout the summer. Look for "slow to bolt" or "heat tolerant" cultivars to extend their season further.

Here's what you'll do:

1. One week before you plan to transplant, cut a "block" around the seedlings (like you'd cut a pan of brownies). This separates the roots.

2. The day before you'll transplant, water the seedlings so that the soil will cling to the roots.

3. When it's time, fill your containers half full with potting mix and moisten.

4. Gently pull apart the blocks, keeping as much soil on the roots as possible. You can separate individual seedlings or small groupings this way.

5. Set a separated root ball on the soil mix (if the roots are long, poke a hole in the soil first). Gently spoon in more soil around the root ball until the container is nearly full—the soil should come up to just beneath the lowest set of leaves. Gently press the soil down around the seedling.

6. Don't forget to label your transplants!

7. Lightly water the seedlings or set in a shallow tray with water for a few hours. Keep out of direct sunlight for the first day or so before returning them to a sunny location.

TIME TO START PLANTING

You might be impatient to get things in the ground, but if you live in a cooler climate, impatience to plant can get the better of you. All those pretty plants the grocery and home-goods stores start to put out can suffer if the overnight temps dip or frost falls. Anything below 24˚F (-4˚C) can be fatal to plants. Keep in mind your frost advisories because anything delicate will need to be brought inside or covered on those chilly nights.

Soil temperature is a good indicator of when you can start planting, particularly for those direct-sow seeds; it should be warm enough to work, ideally between 65˚F and 75˚F (18˚C to 24˚C). Use a soil thermometer (a kitchen thermometer that you'll use just for the garden is fine, too) to check the temperature at night or in the early morning for three days. Go to a depth of 1 to 2 inches (2.5 to 5 cm) for seeds or 4 to 6 inches (10 to 15 cm) for transplants, and leave it for 1 minute. After three days, take the average, and you'll have an idea of when you can start to plant; check the back of your seed packets for ideal soil temps or when you can plant in your zone. Note that raised beds tend to warm up more quickly than ground beds do.

The Old Farmer's Almanac is a terrific resource (both in print and online) to find all sorts of information related to farming and gardening, from annual, eerily accurate weather forecasts to country-style recipes. It's also a great place to consult for your location's first and last frost dates. Similar go-to resources around the world have equally fascinating and locally appropriate information.

TIP: If you have a row garden, keep a strip of grass as a walking path between planting patches. When you mow it, the clippings will automatically act as mulch.

CLEAR THOSE BEDS

Before you can plant, or while you're hardening off transplants (see page 16), you'll need to prepare your space and your soil.

If you're reusing last year's garden beds or garden rows—whether flowers or vegetables—you'll need to clear out any brushy dead plants, newly sprouted weeds, and any other debris, such as faded garden markers, twine, and large stones.

If you're building a fresh, new garden, you'll first need to mow down tall grass and weeds and pull out any stumps, large roots, or rocks. Till the grass that's there to break up the clods of dirt. (To help soften the soil first, cover the area with black plastic or newspaper covered in leaves for a few weeks.)

If you're making a container garden, inspect your pots for cracks or chips and remove any hardened, pot-shaped clumps of old potting soil.

Raised beds don't need to empty your wallet. Cinder blocks work exceptionally well—no tools required. Bonus: you can plant flowers, such as marigolds, in the blocks' holes for a pretty garden border.

ADAPTING PLANTS FOR THE OUTDOORS

To avoid shocking your seedlings, you'll need to acclimate them to the outdoors, if you live in a cooler climate. Called **hardening off**, it's not difficult to do, but it takes some time.

Set out the plants for a few hours in the afternoon in a shady spot—one where they won't get a lot of wind—and bring them in at night. Over four or five days, increase the length of time you keep them out, until they can be out all day. Then move them to a part-sun/part-shade location, or even full-sun if it's not too hot. At this point, you can leave them out overnight if it won't get too cold. Limit how much you water them during this time, but make sure they don't dry out either. Over the course of one to two weeks, you'll notice the stems start to strengthen, or harden, after which time your plants will be ready to transplant.

While hardy crops can tolerate a bit of frost, half-hardy crops should be protected by covering them with a sheet or overturned box at night; tender crops should be brought back inside.

HARDY SEEDLINGS	HALF-HARDY SEEDLINGS	TENDER SEEDLINGS
Broccoli	Beets	Corn (sweet)
Brussels sprouts	Carrots	Cucumbers
Cabbage	Cauliflower	Eggplant
Collards	Celery	Melons
Kale	Chard	Peppers
Leeks	Chinese cabbage	Pumpkins
Onions	Endive	Snap beans
Radishes	Lettuce	Squash
Spinach	Parsnips	Tomatoes
Turnips	Potatoes	Watermelons

TRANSPLANTING TLC

All that attention you gave to your transplants was worth the effort—they're ready to be off on their own! Here's how:

1. Pick a day that's not too sunny or cold. You don't want to shock your baby plants.

2. In your garden, mark off where you want them. You can use stakes and twine or pebbles or even seashells to designate rows. Even if you eyeball the rows, you should mark off the appropriate spacing between plants to give both the foliage and the roots optimal growing conditions.

3. Dig a hole at least as big as the pot your transplant is growing in. If you like, dig another inch deeper and add some compost, covering it with a bit more dirt.

4. Put your hand over the pot, with the plant stem between your thumb and forefinger. Turn it over so your palm is cupping the dirt, and gently remove the pot from the root ball with your other hand.

5. Put the plant in the hole, push dirt into the hole, and give it all a firm pat.

6. Water well for the first week or two, until you see new growth.

7. To avoid damaging roots later on, insert any trellises, stakes, or cages that the plant might need when it grows.

8. Don't forget to label your plants!

Still pay attention to the weather and the location of your garden—at least for the first couple days. A lot of wind, sun, or cold can damage new transplants. You can buy commercial crop or row covers, but something as simple as an inverted paper bag, a milk jug cut in half, or even a tented newspaper can provide enough protection. Anything plastic will heat up, so remove it on a particularly sunny afternoon and replace it at night.

Now is a great time to host an informal plant swap with your neighbors and gardening friends. Ready-to-plant seedlings also make great gifts.

Cut the milk jug or carton in half crosswise and press it into the soil over the plant. Or, cut it in half vertically and cut off the bottom, then push it in the soil next to the plant to block wind or direct sun.

TO TILL OR NOT TO TILL

A tidy garden doesn't necessarily mean one that is weed free. This should come as a relief! Excessively working the soil to keep it "loose" and disrupt new weeds' tiny roots can weaken the soil and harm earthworms and beneficial microbes. To mitigate weeds—and keep your soil healthy—consider topping your garden with organic mulches instead: compost, grass clippings, straw, shredded leaves, and pulled weeds that haven't gone to seed yet (a combination of these mulches is even better).

EARLY SHOWERS BRING HEARTY FLOWERS

It goes without saying that you need to water your seeds and plants; in fact, veggies grow best when their soil is kept moist. Limp or dull leaves can indicate your plants are thirsty, but check the soil to see whether it's damp or dry before dousing them, as wilting could be due to an exceptionally hot day. Dig into the soil—if you have to go deeper than your second knuckle to find moist dark dirt, it's time to bring out the watering can.

The optimal time to water is early morning—this not only gives the water time to soak in (rather than evaporate in the sun), but it also allows time for the leaves to dry before dusk so they don't develop disease. If evening is the only time you can get to your garden, then try to irrigate the base of the plants and not splash the leaves.

Now is a good time to review your watering plan. Are you filling a watering can from the spigot on your house and carrying it to the back of your yard several times? Could you use a soaker hose or a sprinkler? Do you have to drag a hose over, or can you leave it out? If your garden is near a downspout, a rain barrel might be the answer—it's a large vessel that collects rain and it has a spigot where you can attach a hose or let it pour into a watering can.

Jot down thoughts about your watering plan here.

_____

_____

_____

_____

_____

_____

_____

_____

_____

QUITE CONTRARY

Whether you've planted just one thing or your entire garden, if your plants don't grow, it's a little heartbreaking. It's important to observe your plants during the growing season, so you can mitigate loss. Both pest damage and disease can be identified with online resources.

A seed packet will give an approximation of how many days it takes for that seed to germinate. If, after a couple weeks, you're still not seeing much, there could be several reasons why:

- The seeds were too old;
- The seeds were planted too deep;
- The seeds rotted because there wasn't adequate drainage;
- The seeds became a snack for insects, birds, and tiny critters;
- The soil was too cold.

If your leaves have holes or tunnels in them, they've likely become snacks for bugs. Some springtime pests include aphids, cabbage worms, flea beetles, cutworms, leaf miners, root maggots, and slugs.

There are also diseases that might affect seedlings and young plants. Damping off is caused by microorganisms; it either rots the seed before it sprouts or kills off the seedling shortly after it pops through the soil. Club root causes plants to wilt on hot days and recover when it cools, causing leaves to yellow and roots to swell and rot. Leaf spot is just what it sounds like—brown spots on leaves that can reduce the plant's yield.

Once you've identified potential problems, visit your local plant nursery or garden center to inquire about solutions.

Companion planting is putting plants near each other for their mutual benefit. Consider the Native American tradition of planting the Three Sisters together: corn for its tall stalks, beans to climb those stalks, and sprawling squash at the base. The beans add nitrogen to the soil while helping stabilize the corn stalks, and the large squash leaves provide soil coverage to retain moisture and limit weeds. Companion flowers in a vegetable garden can attract pollinators, and many flowers and herbs can deter pests.

TO (pH)ERTILIZE OR NOT TO (pH)ERTILIZE

When your soil is healthy, your plants do better overall. If your plants aren't producing flowers or vegetables, it might be that they're nutrient starved. For new gardens, fertilizers, also called **soil amendments**, should be applied a few weeks before seeds or seedlings go in the ground. Most perennial landscape plants and trees do not need additional fertilizer. The most accurate way to determine what your soil needs is to get it tested in a lab; at-home tests are available, but they might not be as accurate. Lab tests will also measure the pH of your soil—that is, how acidic it is.

Fertilizers get a bad reputation as "big chemical," but at their basic, they're a blend of nitrogen, phosphorous, and potassium. Organic matter (such as compost, shredded leaves, straw, and grass clippings) will add nutrients to your garden over time as worms and other microorganisms break it down. (You can also toss in well-rinsed and broken eggshells.)

Whatever amendments you decide to add, go easy. More is not better. If you go the commercial all-purpose fertilizer route, look for products that are 100 percent natural— you should be able to pronounce all the ingredients. The benefit of these natural amendments is that they won't burn delicate seedlings.

A great example of pH in action is the hydrangea bush. These gorgeous pompom-flowered perennials *can change color* depending on their soil makeup.

SHOUT-OUT TO DIVERSITY

A diverse garden not only looks nice, but it can do better in the long run—that old adage about one rotten apple ruining the bunch holds true for plants. But beyond selecting a rich variety of flowers, herbs, and vegetables, think about how you might branch from "the basics," whether this is your first year gardening or your twentieth year of planting the same old same old.

For example, you could try rainbow carrots, purple asparagus, or yellow tomatoes. Or, if you typically grow pickling cucumbers, why not add one plant of mouse melons (otherwise known as Mexican sour cucumbers)? You could try black sunflowers or bleeding hearts, tulips that are candy striped or chartreuse, or nighttime bloomers like chocolate daisies or evening primrose. You can still plant your favorites, of course, but why not give something new a try?

THINNING THE HERD

Once the seeds you direct sowed start coming up, you'll need to thin the seedlings to encourage their growth. It might seem counterproductive to pull out the plants you've been trying to grow, but overcrowding stunts growth and can cause root veggies to become deformed. The plants left will no longer have to compete for sunlight and soil nutrients.

All you need to do is select your healthiest seedlings and remove the rest. Refer to your seed packets for appropriate spacing between plants, but a good rule of thumb is to give each seedling two finger widths of space. The packet might also indicate when to thin, but it's usually safe to thin when the plants have two true sets of leaves. Damp soil will make the process easier.

WEED IT AND REAP

Weeds are part and parcel of even the most well-tended garden. It could be said that weeds are just plants that grow where you don't want them. That's a kind way of looking at something that, if left unchecked, could crowd out the plants you do want. Follow these tips to be a weeding pro:

Hate weeding? Just do one section at a time or give yourself just 10 or 15 minutes at a crack.

- Smaller weeds are easier to pull.
- Pull them out, roots and all.
- Wet soil is easier to work with.
- Use a garden fork or trowel from time to time if your soil is dry or the weeds are too small (or too stubborn) to pull.
- If you can't get a persistent root out, lop off the weed at its base.
- Cover empty garden spaces, either by mulch, weed barrier, or with leafy, low-lying plants.
- Pull out weeds before they go to seed.

BE A DEADHEAD

To extend the life of your flowering plants, you'll need to give them a little care. Snipping off dead blooms encourages new growth and keeps the plants healthier. Here's how:

Use your garden scissors or small pruning shears to cut off the spent flower. Cut it below the flower, but just above the next set of leaves down the stem. For flowers with a lot of petals, like roses or peonies, wait until nearly all the petals of that flower are spent.

While weeding is easier in damp soil, do not prune or deadhead bushes and large plants when branches are wet, as that can encourage the spread of disease.

If you're looking to add easier flowers to your garden, check the plants' tags for words like "no deadheading," "low maintenance," or "self-cleaning." Options include begonias, calibrachoa (million bells), impatiens, portulaca (moss rose), sedum, and vinca.

YEAR ONE

Gardening is the art that uses
flowers and plants as paint and
the soil and sky as canvas.

-ELIZABETH MURRAY

LET'S GET THIS GARDEN STARTED

Flowers or veggies? Or both? Maybe you have more than one space for planting, or you have enough space for multiple things in one patch. Either way, think about what you want to grow—whether it's a field of poppies or pots of tea-making herbs. In the lists that follow, check whether they're annuals (need replanting each year) or perennials (come back every year), sun- or shade-dwelling, and note the approximate season in which they're at their showiest. Don't limit yourself to a certain number; you will prune your list later.

List of Flower or Ornamental Plants

_____ Season _____ □ Annual □ Perennial □ Sun □ Shade

_____ Season _____ □ Annual □ Perennial □ Sun □ Shade

_____ Season _____ □ Annual □ Perennial □ Sun □ Shade

_____ Season _____ □ Annual □ Perennial □ Sun □ Shade

_____ Season _____ □ Annual □ Perennial □ Sun □ Shade

_____ Season _____ □ Annual □ Perennial □ Sun □ Shade

_____ Season _____ □ Annual □ Perennial □ Sun □ Shade

_____ Season _____ □ Annual □ Perennial □ Sun □ Shade

_____ Season _____ □ Annual □ Perennial □ Sun □ Shade

_____ Season _____ □ Annual □ Perennial □ Sun □ Shade

_____ Season _____ □ Annual □ Perennial □ Sun □ Shade

_____ Season _____ □ Annual □ Perennial □ Sun □ Shade

_____ Season _____ □ Annual □ Perennial □ Sun □ Shade

_____ Season _____ □ Annual □ Perennial □ Sun □ Shade

_____ Season _____ □ Annual □ Perennial □ Sun □ Shade

_____ Season _____ □ Annual □ Perennial □ Sun □ Shade

_____ Season _____ □ Annual □ Perennial □ Sun □ Shade

List of Edible Plants (Herbs, Fruits, Vegetables)

_____ Season _____ ☐ Annual ☐ Perennial ☐ Sun ☐ Shade

_____ Season _____ ☐ Annual ☐ Perennial ☐ Sun ☐ Shade

_____ Season _____ ☐ Annual ☐ Perennial ☐ Sun ☐ Shade

_____ Season _____ ☐ Annual ☐ Perennial ☐ Sun ☐ Shade

_____ Season _____ ☐ Annual ☐ Perennial ☐ Sun ☐ Shade

_____ Season _____ ☐ Annual ☐ Perennial ☐ Sun ☐ Shade

_____ Season _____ ☐ Annual ☐ Perennial ☐ Sun ☐ Shade

_____ Season _____ ☐ Annual ☐ Perennial ☐ Sun ☐ Shade

_____ Season _____ ☐ Annual ☐ Perennial ☐ Sun ☐ Shade

_____ Season _____ ☐ Annual ☐ Perennial ☐ Sun ☐ Shade

_____ Season _____ ☐ Annual ☐ Perennial ☐ Sun ☐ Shade

_____ Season _____ ☐ Annual ☐ Perennial ☐ Sun ☐ Shade

_____ Season _____ ☐ Annual ☐ Perennial ☐ Sun ☐ Shade

_____ Season _____ ☐ Annual ☐ Perennial ☐ Sun ☐ Shade

_____ Season _____ ☐ Annual ☐ Perennial ☐ Sun ☐ Shade

_____ Season _____ ☐ Annual ☐ Perennial ☐ Sun ☐ Shade

_____ Season _____ ☐ Annual ☐ Perennial ☐ Sun ☐ Shade

_____ Season _____ ☐ Annual ☐ Perennial ☐ Sun ☐ Shade

_____ Season _____ ☐ Annual ☐ Perennial ☐ Sun ☐ Shade

_____ Season _____ ☐ Annual ☐ Perennial ☐ Sun ☐ Shade

If this is your first garden, or the idea of starting from scratch is overwhelming, consider a garden theme. Do you love eating caprese salads? You can plant tomatoes and basil in pots. Or plan for a rainbow of flowers, one type in each color. Narrow your scope, and you'll find your way.

MAKE A LIST, CHECK IT TWICE

Now select which plants you can actually fit in your garden. (If you can't fit in everything you dreamed of this year, take heart: there's always next.) Finalizing your plants will save your sanity—and your wallet.

Review your lists on the previous pages and write down your plant choices, starting with your top picks. Note which you'll sow directly in your garden, which you'll start indoors or buy as seedlings, and which you'll wait to buy as larger plants. Jot down approximate date(s) that you will need to direct sow or start seeds as well as what you'll need for each of them (e.g., cages for tomatoes, a trellis for cucumbers, ornamental mulch or stones to place around flowers, seed-starter pots and dirt). If you're unsure of anything, start your research online (Cooperative Extension Services are great), in seed and plant catalogs, and in garden centers.

_____ plant date _____
☐ direct sow ☐ start as seeds ☐ buy seedlings ☐ buy plants

_____ plant date _____
☐ direct sow ☐ start as seeds ☐ buy seedlings ☐ buy plants

_____ plant date _____
☐ direct sow ☐ start as seeds ☐ buy seedlings ☐ buy plants

_____ plant date _____
☐ direct sow ☐ start as seeds ☐ buy seedlings ☐ buy plants

_____ plant date _____
☐ direct sow ☐ start as seeds ☐ buy seedlings ☐ buy plants

_____ plant date _____
☐ direct sow ☐ start as seeds ☐ buy seedlings ☐ buy plants

_____ plant date _____
☐ direct sow ☐ start as seeds ☐ buy seedlings ☐ buy plants

_____ plant date _____
☐ direct sow ☐ start as seeds ☐ buy seedlings ☐ buy plants

_____ plant date ____ _____

☐ direct sow ☐ start as seeds ☐ buy seedlings ☐ buy plants

_____ plant date _____

☐ direct sow ☐ start as seeds ☐ buy seedlings ☐ buy plants

_____ plant date _____

☐ direct sow ☐ start as seeds ☐ buy seedlings ☐ buy plants

_____ plant date _____

☐ direct sow ☐ start as seeds ☐ buy seedlings ☐ buy plants

_____ plant date _____

☐ direct sow ☐ start as seeds ☐ buy seedlings ☐ buy plants

_____ plant date _____

☐ direct sow ☐ start as seeds ☐ buy seedlings ☐ buy plants

_____ plant date _____

☐ direct sow ☐ start as seeds ☐ buy seedlings ☐ buy plants

_____ plant date _____

☐ direct sow ☐ start as seeds ☐ buy seedlings ☐ buy plants

_____ plant date _____

☐ direct sow ☐ start as seeds ☐ buy seedlings ☐ buy plants

_____ plant date _____

☐ direct sow ☐ start as seeds ☐ buy seedlings ☐ buy plants

_____ plant date _____

☐ direct sow ☐ start as seeds ☐ buy seedlings ☐ buy plants

_____ plant date _____

☐ direct sow ☐ start as seeds ☐ buy seedlings ☐ buy plants

_____ plant date _____

☐ direct sow ☐ start as seeds ☐ buy seedlings ☐ buy plants

WHAT GOES WHERE

Maybe you're planning on part flowers and part vegetables. Or you have a certain number of rows for various seedlings. Or you're planting early crops that will become summer or cold-weather crops later on.

Using the measurements you recorded on page 6, map out your garden on these pages. Start with the plants at the top of your list from page 28 to make sure you have enough room for them. You might find that you have to narrow your lists even more—or that you have room to add others.

SAVE THOSE TAGS

Every plant you buy comes with a little label or tag with care instructions that includes sun and water preference. Use these pages to tape them in so you always have them. If the tags are dirty, or you'd rather not paste them here, then jot down some care instructions (and use the tags to label your plants).

YEAR ONE

YEAR TWO

YEAR THREE

YEAR FOUR

YEAR FIVE

PLANTS LOG

In order to learn from your garden this year so you can improve it—and how you manage it—next year, it's essential that you keep track of what you've planted and when. It's the only way to know when transplants and seeds will do their best in *your* yard. Maybe you'll put seedlings out too early or in a location that receives too much afternoon sun. Or you'll put your seeds in the ground too late for them to produce much. Remember that seed packets and plant tags are just guidelines—your yard is unique. Keep a running list of your plants in these pages. Make notes about any troubles or successes, whether you'll plant something again, or anything else you might keep or change up.

PLANT NAME/CULTIVAR _____

☐ Seed ☐ Bulb ☐ Root ☐ Seedling ☐ Plant

Date bought _____ From where _____

Date planted _____

Where planted _____

Date germinated _____

Date (trans)planted _____

Soil amendments _____

Insect damage or disease _____

Date(s) harvested _____

Watering frequency _____

Notes _____

PLANT NAME/CULTIVAR _____

☐ Seed ☐ Bulb ☐ Root ☐ Seedling ☐ Plant

Date bought _____ From where _____

Date planted _____

Where planted _____

Date germinated _____

Date (trans)planted _____

Soil amendments _____

_____

Insect damage or disease _____

_____

Date(s) harvested _____

_____

Watering frequency _____

_____

Notes _____

_____

_____

_____

_____

YEAR ONE

YEAR TWO

YEAR THREE

YEAR FOUR

YEAR FIVE

PLANT NAME/CULTIVAR _____

☐ Seed   ☐ Bulb   ☐ Root   ☐ Seedling   ☐ Plant

Date bought _____ From where _____

Date planted _____

Where planted _____

Date germinated _____

Date (trans)planted _____

Soil amendments _____

_____

Insect damage or disease _____

_____

Date(s) harvested _____

_____

Watering frequency _____

_____

Notes _____

_____

_____

_____

_____

PLANT NAME/CULTIVAR _____

☐ Seed   ☐ Bulb   ☐ Root   ☐ Seedling   ☐ Plant

Date bought _____ From where _____

Date planted _____

Where planted _____

Date germinated _____

Date (trans)planted _____

Soil amendments _____

_____

Insect damage or disease _____

_____

Date(s) harvested _____

_____

Watering frequency _____

_____

Notes _____

_____

_____

_____

_____

PLANT NAME/CULTIVAR _____

☐ Seed   ☐ Bulb   ☐ Root   ☐ Seedling   ☐ Plant

Date bought _____ From where _____

Date planted _____

Where planted _____

Date germinated _____

Date (trans)planted _____

Soil amendments _____

_____

Insect damage or disease _____

_____

Date(s) harvested _____

_____

Watering frequency _____

_____

Notes _____

_____

_____

_____

_____

PLANT NAME/CULTIVAR _____

☐ Seed ☐ Bulb ☐ Root ☐ Seedling ☐ Plant

Date bought _____ From where _____

Date planted _____

Where planted _____

Date germinated _____

Date (trans)planted _____

Soil amendments _____

_____

Insect damage or disease _____

_____

Date(s) harvested _____

_____

Watering frequency _____

_____

Notes _____

_____

_____

_____

_____

PLANT NAME/CULTIVAR _____

☐ Seed   ☐ Bulb   ☐ Root   ☐ Seedling   ☐ Plant

Date bought _____ From where _____

Date planted _____

Where planted _____

Date germinated _____

Date (trans)planted _____

Soil amendments _____

_____

Insect damage or disease _____

_____

Date(s) harvested _____

_____

Watering frequency _____

_____

Notes _____

_____

_____

_____

_____

PLANT NAME/CULTIVAR _____

☐ Seed   ☐ Bulb   ☐ Root   ☐ Seedling   ☐ Plant

Date bought _____ From where _____

Date planted _____

Where planted _____

Date germinated _____

Date (trans)planted _____

Soil amendments _____

_____

Insect damage or disease _____

_____

Date(s) harvested _____

_____

Watering frequency _____

_____

Notes _____

_____

_____

_____

_____

PLANT NAME/CULTIVAR _____

☐ Seed   ☐ Bulb   ☐ Root   ☐ Seedling   ☐ Plant

Date bought _____ From where _____

Date planted _____

Where planted _____

Date germinated _____

Date (trans)planted _____

Soil amendments _____

_____

Insect damage or disease _____

_____

Date(s) harvested _____

_____

Watering frequency _____

_____

Notes _____

_____

_____

_____

_____

PLANT NAME/CULTIVAR _____

☐ Seed ☐ Bulb ☐ Root ☐ Seedling ☐ Plant

Date bought _____ From where _____

Date planted _____

Where planted _____

Date germinated _____

Date (trans)planted _____

Soil amendments _____

_____

Insect damage or disease _____

_____

Date(s) harvested _____

_____

Watering frequency _____

_____

Notes _____

_____

_____

_____

PLANT NAME/CULTIVAR _____

☐ Seed ☐ Bulb ☐ Root ☐ Seedling ☐ Plant

Date bought _____ From where _____

Date planted _____

Where planted _____

Date germinated _____

Date (trans)planted _____

Soil amendments _____

Insect damage or disease _____

Date(s) harvested _____

Watering frequency _____

Notes _____

PLANT NAME/CULTIVAR _____

☐ Seed   ☐ Bulb   ☐ Root   ☐ Seedling   ☐ Plant

Date bought _____ From where _____

Date planted _____

Where planted _____

Date germinated _____

Date (trans)planted _____

Soil amendments _____

_____

Insect damage or disease _____

_____

Date(s) harvested _____

_____

Watering frequency _____

_____

Notes _____

_____

_____

_____

_____

PLANT NAME/CULTIVAR _____

☐ Seed ☐ Bulb ☐ Root ☐ Seedling ☐ Plant

Date bought _____ From where _____

Date planted _____

Where planted _____

Date germinated _____

Date (trans)planted _____

Soil amendments _____

_____

Insect damage or disease _____

_____

Date(s) harvested _____

_____

Watering frequency _____

_____

Notes _____

_____

_____

_____

_____

PLANT NAME/CULTIVAR _____

☐ Seed   ☐ Bulb   ☐ Root   ☐ Seedling   ☐ Plant

Date bought _____ From where _____

Date planted _____

Where planted _____

Date germinated _____

Date (trans)planted _____

Soil amendments _____

_____

Insect damage or disease _____

_____

Date(s) harvested _____

_____

Watering frequency _____

_____

Notes _____

_____

_____

_____

PLANT NAME/CULTIVAR _____

☐ Seed ☐ Bulb ☐ Root ☐ Seedling ☐ Plant

Date bought _____ From where _____

Date planted _____

Where planted _____

Date germinated _____

Date (trans)planted _____

Soil amendments _____

_____

Insect damage or disease _____

_____

Date(s) harvested _____

_____

Watering frequency _____

_____

Notes _____

_____

_____

_____

_____

PLANT NAME/CULTIVAR _____

☐ Seed   ☐ Bulb   ☐ Root   ☐ Seedling   ☐ Plant

Date bought _____ From where _____

Date planted _____

Where planted _____

Date germinated _____

Date (trans)planted _____

Soil amendments _____

_____

Insect damage or disease _____

_____

Date(s) harvested _____

_____

Watering frequency _____

_____

Notes _____

_____

_____

_____

_____

PLANT NAME/CULTIVAR _____

☐ Seed ☐ Bulb ☐ Root ☐ Seedling ☐ Plant

Date bought _____ From where _____

Date planted _____

Where planted _____

Date germinated _____

Date (trans)planted _____

Soil amendments _____

_____

Insect damage or disease _____

_____

Date(s) harvested _____

_____

Watering frequency _____

_____

Notes _____

_____

_____

_____

_____

PLANT NAME/CULTIVAR _____

☐ Seed   ☐ Bulb   ☐ Root   ☐ Seedling   ☐ Plant

Date bought _____ From where _____

Date planted _____

Where planted _____

Date germinated _____

Date (trans)planted _____

Soil amendments _____

_____

Insect damage or disease _____

_____

Date(s) harvested _____

_____

Watering frequency _____

_____

Notes _____

_____

_____

_____

_____

YEAR TWO

(Gardening) is the purest
of human pleasures.

-FRANCIS BACON,
"OF GARDENS"

LET'S GET THIS GARDEN STARTED

Think about what you want to grow. In the lists that follow, check whether they're annuals or perennials, sun- or shade-dwelling, and note the approximate season in which they're at their showiest. Don't limit yourself to a certain number; you will prune your list later.

List of Flower or Ornamental Plants

_____ Season _____ □ Annual □ Perennial □ Sun □ Shade

_____ Season _____ □ Annual □ Perennial □ Sun □ Shade

_____ Season _____ □ Annual □ Perennial □ Sun □ Shade

_____ Season _____ □ Annual □ Perennial □ Sun □ Shade

_____ Season _____ □ Annual □ Perennial □ Sun □ Shade

_____ Season _____ □ Annual □ Perennial □ Sun □ Shade

_____ Season _____ □ Annual □ Perennial □ Sun □ Shade

_____ Season _____ □ Annual □ Perennial □ Sun □ Shade

_____ Season _____ □ Annual □ Perennial □ Sun □ Shade

_____ Season _____ □ Annual □ Perennial □ Sun □ Shade

_____ Season _____ □ Annual □ Perennial □ Sun □ Shade

_____ Season _____ □ Annual □ Perennial □ Sun □ Shade

_____ Season _____ □ Annual □ Perennial □ Sun □ Shade

_____ Season _____ □ Annual □ Perennial □ Sun □ Shade

_____ Season _____ □ Annual □ Perennial □ Sun □ Shade

_____ Season _____ □ Annual □ Perennial □ Sun □ Shade

_____ Season _____ □ Annual □ Perennial □ Sun □ Shade

_____ Season _____ □ Annual □ Perennial □ Sun □ Shade

_____ Season _____ □ Annual □ Perennial □ Sun □ Shade

List of Edible Plants (Herbs, Fruits, Vegetables)

_____ Season _____ ☐ Annual ☐ Perennial ☐ Sun ☐ Shade

_____ Season _____ ☐ Annual ☐ Perennial ☐ Sun ☐ Shade

_____ Season _____ ☐ Annual ☐ Perennial ☐ Sun ☐ Shade

_____ Season _____ ☐ Annual ☐ Perennial ☐ Sun ☐ Shade

_____ Season _____ ☐ Annual ☐ Perennial ☐ Sun ☐ Shade

_____ Season _____ ☐ Annual ☐ Perennial ☐ Sun ☐ Shade

_____ Season _____ ☐ Annual ☐ Perennial ☐ Sun ☐ Shade

_____ Season _____ ☐ Annual ☐ Perennial ☐ Sun ☐ Shade

_____ Season _____ ☐ Annual ☐ Perennial ☐ Sun ☐ Shade

_____ Season _____ ☐ Annual ☐ Perennial ☐ Sun ☐ Shade

_____ Season _____ ☐ Annual ☐ Perennial ☐ Sun ☐ Shade

_____ Season _____ ☐ Annual ☐ Perennial ☐ Sun ☐ Shade

_____ Season _____ ☐ Annual ☐ Perennial ☐ Sun ☐ Shade

_____ Season _____ ☐ Annual ☐ Perennial ☐ Sun ☐ Shade

_____ Season _____ ☐ Annual ☐ Perennial ☐ Sun ☐ Shade

_____ Season _____ ☐ Annual ☐ Perennial ☐ Sun ☐ Shade

_____ Season _____ ☐ Annual ☐ Perennial ☐ Sun ☐ Shade

_____ Season _____ ☐ Annual ☐ Perennial ☐ Sun ☐ Shade

_____ Season _____ ☐ Annual ☐ Perennial ☐ Sun ☐ Shade

_____ Season _____ ☐ Annual ☐ Perennial ☐ Sun ☐ Shade

_____ Season _____ ☐ Annual ☐ Perennial ☐ Sun ☐ Shade

_____ Season _____ ☐ Annual ☐ Perennial ☐ Sun ☐ Shade

_____ Season _____ ☐ Annual ☐ Perennial ☐ Sun ☐ Shade

MAKE A LIST, CHECK IT TWICE

Review your lists on the previous pages and write down your plant choices, starting with your top picks. Note which you'll sow directly in your garden, which you'll start indoors or buy as seedlings, and which you'll wait to buy as larger plants. Jot down approximate date(s) that you will need to direct sow or start seeds as well as what you'll need for each of them. Complete an inventory of what you saved from last year and place a checkmark next to any seeds or bulbs you can still use.

_____ plant date _____

☐ direct sow ☐ start as seeds ☐ buy seedlings ☐ buy plants

_____ plant date _____

☐ direct sow ☐ start as seeds ☐ buy seedlings ☐ buy plants

_____ plant date _____

☐ direct sow ☐ start as seeds ☐ buy seedlings ☐ buy plants

_____ plant date _____

☐ direct sow ☐ start as seeds ☐ buy seedlings ☐ buy plants

_____ plant date _____

☐ direct sow ☐ start as seeds ☐ buy seedlings ☐ buy plants

_____ plant date _____

☐ direct sow ☐ start as seeds ☐ buy seedlings ☐ buy plants

_____ plant date _____

☐ direct sow ☐ start as seeds ☐ buy seedlings ☐ buy plants

_____ plant date _____

☐ direct sow ☐ start as seeds ☐ buy seedlings ☐ buy plants

_____ plant date _____

☐ direct sow ☐ start as seeds ☐ buy seedlings ☐ buy plants

_____ plant date _____

☐ direct sow ☐ start as seeds ☐ buy seedlings ☐ buy plants

_____ plant date _____

□ direct sow □ start as seeds □ buy seedlings □ buy plants

_____ plant date _____

□ direct sow □ start as seeds □ buy seedlings □ buy plants

_____ plant date _____

□ direct sow □ start as seeds □ buy seedlings □ buy plants

_____ plant date _____

□ direct sow □ start as seeds □ buy seedlings □ buy plants

_____ plant date _____

□ direct sow □ start as seeds □ buy seedlings □ buy plants

_____ plant date _____

□ direct sow □ start as seeds □ buy seedlings □ buy plants

_____ plant date _____

□ direct sow □ start as seeds □ buy seedlings □ buy plants

_____ plant date _____

□ direct sow □ start as seeds □ buy seedlings □ buy plants

_____ plant date _____

□ direct sow □ start as seeds □ buy seedlings □ buy plants

_____ plant date _____

□ direct sow □ start as seeds □ buy seedlings □ buy plants

_____ plant date _____

□ direct sow □ start as seeds □ buy seedlings □ buy plants

_____ plant date _____

□ direct sow □ start as seeds □ buy seedlings □ buy plants

_____ plant date _____

□ direct sow □ start as seeds □ buy seedlings □ buy plants

_____ plant date _____

□ direct sow □ start as seeds □ buy seedlings □ buy plants

WHAT GOES WHERE

Map out your garden(s) here. Start with the plants at the top of your list from page 55 to make sure you have enough room for them. You might find that you have to narrow your lists even more—or that you have room to add others.

SAVE THOSE TAGS

Every plant you buy comes with a little label or tag with care instructions that includes sun and water preference. Use these pages to tape them in so you always have them. If the tags are dirty, or you'd rather not paste them here, then jot down some care instructions (and use the tags to label your plants).

PLANTS LOG

Keep a running list of your plants in these pages. Make notes about any troubles or successes, whether you'll plant something again, or anything else you might keep or change up.

PLANT NAME/CULTIVAR _____

☐ Seed   ☐ Bulb   ☐ Root   ☐ Seedling   ☐ Plant

Date bought _____ From where _____

Date planted _____

Where planted _____

Date germinated _____

Date (trans)planted _____

Soil amendments _____

Insect damage or disease _____

_____

Date(s) harvested _____

_____

Watering frequency _____

_____

Notes _____

_____

PLANT NAME/CULTIVAR _____

☐ Seed ☐ Bulb ☐ Root ☐ Seedling ☐ Plant

Date bought _____ From where _____

Date planted _____

Where planted _____

Date germinated _____

Date (trans)planted _____

Soil amendments _____
_____

Insect damage or disease _____
_____

Date(s) harvested _____
_____

Watering frequency _____
_____

Notes _____
_____
_____
_____

PLANT NAME/CULTIVAR _____

☐ Seed ☐ Bulb ☐ Root ☐ Seedling ☐ Plant

Date bought _____ From where _____

Date planted _____

Where planted _____

Date germinated _____

Date (trans)planted _____

Soil amendments _____

_____

Insect damage or disease _____

_____

Date(s) harvested _____

_____

Watering frequency _____

_____

Notes _____

_____

_____

_____

PLANT NAME/CULTIVAR _____

☐ Seed   ☐ Bulb   ☐ Root   ☐ Seedling   ☐ Plant

Date bought _____ From where _____

Date planted _____

Where planted _____

Date germinated _____

Date (trans)planted _____

Soil amendments _____

_____

Insect damage or disease _____

_____

Date(s) harvested _____

_____

Watering frequency _____

_____

Notes _____

_____

_____

_____

_____

PLANT NAME/CULTIVAR _____

☐ Seed ☐ Bulb ☐ Root ☐ Seedling ☐ Plant

Date bought _____ From where _____

Date planted _____

Where planted _____

Date germinated _____

Date (trans)planted _____

Soil amendments _____
_____

Insect damage or disease _____
_____

Date(s) harvested _____
_____

Watering frequency _____
_____

Notes _____
_____
_____
_____

PLANT NAME/CULTIVAR _____

☐ Seed   ☐ Bulb   ☐ Root   ☐ Seedling   ☐ Plant

Date bought _____ From where _____

Date planted _____

Where planted _____

Date germinated _____

Date (trans)planted _____

Soil amendments _____

_____

Insect damage or disease _____

_____

Date(s) harvested _____

_____

Watering frequency _____

_____

Notes _____

_____

_____

_____

_____

PLANT NAME/CULTIVAR _____

☐ Seed   ☐ Bulb   ☐ Root   ☐ Seedling   ☐ Plant

Date bought _____ From where _____

Date planted _____

Where planted _____

Date germinated _____

Date (trans)planted _____

Soil amendments _____

_____

Insect damage or disease _____

_____

Date(s) harvested _____

_____

Watering frequency _____

_____

Notes _____

_____

_____

_____

_____

PLANT NAME/CULTIVAR _____

☐ Seed   ☐ Bulb   ☐ Root   ☐ Seedling   ☐ Plant

Date bought _____ From where _____

Date planted _____

Where planted _____

Date germinated _____

Date (trans)planted _____

Soil amendments _____

_____

Insect damage or disease _____

_____

Date(s) harvested _____

_____

Watering frequency _____

_____

Notes _____

_____

_____

_____

_____

PLANT NAME/CULTIVAR _____

☐ Seed   ☐ Bulb   ☐ Root   ☐ Seedling   ☐ Plant

Date bought _____ From where _____

Date planted _____

Where planted _____

Date germinated _____

Date (trans)planted _____

Soil amendments _____

_____

Insect damage or disease _____

_____

Date(s) harvested _____

_____

Watering frequency _____

_____

Notes _____

_____

_____

_____

_____

PLANT NAME/CULTIVAR _____

☐ Seed ☐ Bulb ☐ Root ☐ Seedling ☐ Plant

Date bought _____ From where _____

Date planted _____

Where planted _____

Date germinated _____

Date (trans)planted _____

Soil amendments _____

_____

Insect damage or disease _____

_____

Date(s) harvested _____

_____

Watering frequency _____

_____

Notes _____

_____

_____

_____

_____

PLANT NAME/CULTIVAR _____

☐ Seed   ☐ Bulb   ☐ Root   ☐ Seedling   ☐ Plant

Date bought _____ From where _____

Date planted _____

Where planted _____

Date germinated _____

Date (trans)planted _____

Soil amendments _____

_____

Insect damage or disease _____

_____

Date(s) harvested _____

_____

Watering frequency _____

_____

Notes _____

_____

_____

_____

_____

PLANT NAME/CULTIVAR _____

☐ Seed   ☐ Bulb   ☐ Root   ☐ Seedling   ☐ Plant

Date bought _____ From where _____

Date planted _____

Where planted _____

Date germinated _____

Date (trans)planted _____

Soil amendments _____

_____

Insect damage or disease _____

_____

Date(s) harvested _____

_____

Watering frequency _____

_____

Notes _____

_____

_____

_____

_____

PLANT NAME/CULTIVAR _____

☐ Seed　　☐ Bulb　　☐ Root　　☐ Seedling　　☐ Plant

Date bought _____ From where _____

Date planted _____

Where planted _____

Date germinated _____

Date (trans)planted _____

Soil amendments _____

_____

Insect damage or disease _____

_____

Date(s) harvested _____

_____

Watering frequency _____

_____

Notes _____

_____

_____

_____

_____

PLANT NAME/CULTIVAR _____

☐ Seed   ☐ Bulb   ☐ Root   ☐ Seedling   ☐ Plant

Date bought _____ From where _____

Date planted _____

Where planted _____

Date germinated _____

Date (trans)planted _____

Soil amendments _____
_____

Insect damage or disease _____
_____

Date(s) harvested _____
_____

Watering frequency _____
_____

Notes _____
_____
_____
_____

PLANT NAME/CULTIVAR _____

☐ Seed ☐ Bulb ☐ Root ☐ Seedling ☐ Plant

Date bought _____ From where _____

Date planted _____

Where planted _____

Date germinated _____

Date (trans)planted _____

Soil amendments _____

_____

Insect damage or disease _____

_____

Date(s) harvested _____

_____

Watering frequency _____

_____

Notes _____

_____

_____

_____

_____

YEAR ONE

YEAR TWO

YEAR THREE

YEAR FOUR

YEAR FIVE

PLANT NAME/CULTIVAR _____

☐ Seed ☐ Bulb ☐ Root ☐ Seedling ☐ Plant

Date bought _____ From where _____

Date planted _____

Where planted _____

Date germinated _____

Date (trans)planted _____

Soil amendments _____

_____

Insect damage or disease _____

_____

Date(s) harvested _____

_____

Watering frequency _____

_____

Notes _____

_____

_____

_____

_____

PLANT NAME/CULTIVAR _____

☐ Seed ☐ Bulb ☐ Root ☐ Seedling ☐ Plant

Date bought _____ From where _____

Date planted _____

Where planted _____

Date germinated _____

Date (trans)planted _____

Soil amendments _____

_____

Insect damage or disease _____

_____

Date(s) harvested _____

_____

Watering frequency _____

_____

Notes _____

_____

_____

_____

_____

PLANT NAME/CULTIVAR _____

☐ Seed ☐ Bulb ☐ Root ☐ Seedling ☐ Plant

Date bought _____ From where _____

Date planted _____

Where planted _____

Date germinated _____

Date (trans)planted _____

Soil amendments _____

_____

Insect damage or disease _____

_____

Date(s) harvested _____

_____

Watering frequency _____

_____

Notes _____

_____

_____

_____

_____

YEAR THREE

In all things of nature there is
something of the marvelous.

-ARISTOTLE

LET'S GET THIS GARDEN STARTED

Think about what you want to grow. In the lists that follow, check whether they're annuals or perennials, sun- or shade-dwelling, and note the approximate season in which they're at their showiest. Don't limit yourself to a certain number; you will prune your list later.

List of Flower or Ornamental Plants

_____ Season _____ ☐ Annual ☐ Perennial ☐ Sun ☐ Shade

_____ Season _____ ☐ Annual ☐ Perennial ☐ Sun ☐ Shade

_____ Season _____ ☐ Annual ☐ Perennial ☐ Sun ☐ Shade

_____ Season _____ ☐ Annual ☐ Perennial ☐ Sun ☐ Shade

_____ Season _____ ☐ Annual ☐ Perennial ☐ Sun ☐ Shade

_____ Season _____ ☐ Annual ☐ Perennial ☐ Sun ☐ Shade

_____ Season _____ ☐ Annual ☐ Perennial ☐ Sun ☐ Shade

_____ Season _____ ☐ Annual ☐ Perennial ☐ Sun ☐ Shade

_____ Season _____ ☐ Annual ☐ Perennial ☐ Sun ☐ Shade

_____ Season _____ ☐ Annual ☐ Perennial ☐ Sun ☐ Shade

_____ Season _____ ☐ Annual ☐ Perennial ☐ Sun ☐ Shade

_____ Season _____ ☐ Annual ☐ Perennial ☐ Sun ☐ Shade

_____ Season _____ ☐ Annual ☐ Perennial ☐ Sun ☐ Shade

_____ Season _____ ☐ Annual ☐ Perennial ☐ Sun ☐ Shade

_____ Season _____ ☐ Annual ☐ Perennial ☐ Sun ☐ Shade

_____ Season _____ ☐ Annual ☐ Perennial ☐ Sun ☐ Shade

_____ Season _____ ☐ Annual ☐ Perennial ☐ Sun ☐ Shade

_____ Season _____ ☐ Annual ☐ Perennial ☐ Sun ☐ Shade

List of Edible Plants (Herbs, Fruits, Vegetables)

_____ Season _____ ☐ Annual ☐ Perennial ☐ Sun ☐ Shade

_____ Season _____ ☐ Annual ☐ Perennial ☐ Sun ☐ Shade

_____ Season _____ ☐ Annual ☐ Perennial ☐ Sun ☐ Shade

_____ Season _____ ☐ Annual ☐ Perennial ☐ Sun ☐ Shade

_____ Season _____ ☐ Annual ☐ Perennial ☐ Sun ☐ Shade

_____ Season _____ ☐ Annual ☐ Perennial ☐ Sun ☐ Shade

_____ Season _____ ☐ Annual ☐ Perennial ☐ Sun ☐ Shade

_____ Season _____ ☐ Annual ☐ Perennial ☐ Sun ☐ Shade

_____ Season _____ ☐ Annual ☐ Perennial ☐ Sun ☐ Shade

_____ Season _____ ☐ Annual ☐ Perennial ☐ Sun ☐ Shade

_____ Season _____ ☐ Annual ☐ Perennial ☐ Sun ☐ Shade

_____ Season _____ ☐ Annual ☐ Perennial ☐ Sun ☐ Shade

_____ Season _____ ☐ Annual ☐ Perennial ☐ Sun ☐ Shade

_____ Season _____ ☐ Annual ☐ Perennial ☐ Sun ☐ Shade

_____ Season _____ ☐ Annual ☐ Perennial ☐ Sun ☐ Shade

_____ Season _____ ☐ Annual ☐ Perennial ☐ Sun ☐ Shade

_____ Season _____ ☐ Annual ☐ Perennial ☐ Sun ☐ Shade

_____ Season _____ ☐ Annual ☐ Perennial ☐ Sun ☐ Shade

_____ Season _____ ☐ Annual ☐ Perennial ☐ Sun ☐ Shade

_____ Season _____ ☐ Annual ☐ Perennial ☐ Sun ☐ Shade

_____ Season _____ ☐ Annual ☐ Perennial ☐ Sun ☐ Shade

_____ Season _____ ☐ Annual ☐ Perennial ☐ Sun ☐ Shade

_____ Season _____ ☐ Annual ☐ Perennial ☐ Sun ☐ Shade

MAKE A LIST, CHECK IT TWICE

Review your lists on the previous pages and write down your plant choices, starting with your top picks. Note which you'll sow directly in your garden, which you'll start indoors or buy as seedlings, and which you'll wait to buy as larger plants. Jot down approximate date(s) that you will need to direct sow or start seeds as well as what you'll need for each of them. Complete an inventory of what you saved from last year and place a checkmark next to any seeds or bulbs you can still use.

_____ plant date _____
☐ direct sow ☐ start as seeds ☐ buy seedlings ☐ buy plants

_____ plant date _____
☐ direct sow ☐ start as seeds ☐ buy seedlings ☐ buy plants

_____ plant date _____
☐ direct sow ☐ start as seeds ☐ buy seedlings ☐ buy plants

_____ plant date _____
☐ direct sow ☐ start as seeds ☐ buy seedlings ☐ buy plants

_____ plant date _____
☐ direct sow ☐ start as seeds ☐ buy seedlings ☐ buy plants

_____ plant date _____
☐ direct sow ☐ start as seeds ☐ buy seedlings ☐ buy plants

_____ plant date _____
☐ direct sow ☐ start as seeds ☐ buy seedlings ☐ buy plants

_____ plant date _____
☐ direct sow ☐ start as seeds ☐ buy seedlings ☐ buy plants

_____ plant date _____
☐ direct sow ☐ start as seeds ☐ buy seedlings ☐ buy plants

_____ plant date _____
☐ direct sow ☐ start as seeds ☐ buy seedlings ☐ buy plants

_____ plant date _____
☐ direct sow ☐ start as seeds ☐ buy seedlings ☐ buy plants

_____ plant date _____
☐ direct sow ☐ start as seeds ☐ buy seedlings ☐ buy plants

_____ plant date _____
☐ direct sow ☐ start as seeds ☐ buy seedlings ☐ buy plants

_____ plant date _____
☐ direct sow ☐ start as seeds ☐ buy seedlings ☐ buy plants

_____ plant date _____
☐ direct sow ☐ start as seeds ☐ buy seedlings ☐ buy plants

_____ plant date _____
☐ direct sow ☐ start as seeds ☐ buy seedlings ☐ buy plants

_____ plant date _____
☐ direct sow ☐ start as seeds ☐ buy seedlings ☐ buy plants

_____ plant date _____
☐ direct sow ☐ start as seeds ☐ buy seedlings ☐ buy plants

_____ plant date _____
☐ direct sow ☐ start as seeds ☐ buy seedlings ☐ buy plants

_____ plant date _____
☐ direct sow ☐ start as seeds ☐ buy seedlings ☐ buy plants

_____ plant date _____
☐ direct sow ☐ start as seeds ☐ buy seedlings ☐ buy plants

_____ plant date _____
☐ direct sow ☐ start as seeds ☐ buy seedlings ☐ buy plants

_____ plant date _____
☐ direct sow ☐ start as seeds ☐ buy seedlings ☐ buy plants

_____ plant date _____
☐ direct sow ☐ start as seeds ☐ buy seedlings ☐ buy plants

WHAT GOES WHERE

Map out your garden(s) here. Start with the plants at the top of your list from page 82 to make sure you have enough room for them. You might find that you have to narrow your lists even more—or that you have room to add others.

SAVE THOSE TAGS

Every plant you buy comes with a little label or tag with care instructions that includes sun and water preference. Use these pages to tape them in so you always have them. If the tags are dirty, or you'd rather not paste them here, then jot down some care instructions (and use the tags to label your plants).

PLANTS LOG

Keep a running list of your plants in these pages. Make notes about any troubles or successes, whether you'll plant something again, or anything else you might keep or change up.

PLANT NAME/CULTIVAR _____

☐ Seed ☐ Bulb ☐ Root ☐ Seedling ☐ Plant

Date bought _____ From where _____

Date planted _____

Where planted _____

Date germinated _____

Date (trans)planted _____

Soil amendments _____

Insect damage or disease _____

_____

Date(s) harvested _____

_____

Watering frequency _____

_____

Notes _____

_____

PLANT NAME/CULTIVAR _____

☐ Seed   ☐ Bulb   ☐ Root   ☐ Seedling   ☐ Plant

Date bought _____ From where _____

Date planted _____

Where planted _____

Date germinated _____

Date (trans)planted _____

Soil amendments _____

_____

Insect damage or disease _____

_____

Date(s) harvested _____

_____

Watering frequency _____

_____

Notes _____

_____

_____

_____

_____

PLANT NAME/CULTIVAR _____

☐ Seed   ☐ Bulb   ☐ Root   ☐ Seedling   ☐ Plant

Date bought _____ From where _____

Date planted _____

Where planted _____

Date germinated _____

Date (trans)planted _____

Soil amendments _____

_____

Insect damage or disease _____

_____

Date(s) harvested _____

_____

Watering frequency _____

_____

Notes _____

_____

_____

_____

PLANT NAME/CULTIVAR _____

☐ Seed   ☐ Bulb   ☐ Root   ☐ Seedling   ☐ Plant

Date bought _____ From where _____

Date planted _____

Where planted _____

Date germinated _____

Date (trans)planted _____

Soil amendments _____

_____

Insect damage or disease _____

_____

Date(s) harvested _____

_____

Watering frequency _____

_____

Notes _____

_____

_____

_____

_____

PLANT NAME/CULTIVAR _____

☐ Seed   ☐ Bulb   ☐ Root   ☐ Seedling   ☐ Plant

Date bought _____ From where _____

Date planted _____

Where planted _____

Date germinated _____

Date (trans)planted _____

Soil amendments _____
_____

Insect damage or disease _____
_____

Date(s) harvested _____
_____

Watering frequency _____
_____

Notes _____
_____
_____
_____
_____

PLANT NAME/CULTIVAR _____

☐ Seed   ☐ Bulb   ☐ Root   ☐ Seedling   ☐ Plant

Date bought _____ From where _____

Date planted _____

Where planted _____

Date germinated _____

Date (trans)planted _____

Soil amendments _____

_____

Insect damage or disease _____

_____

Date(s) harvested _____

_____

Watering frequency _____

_____

Notes _____

_____

_____

_____

PLANT NAME/CULTIVAR _____

☐ Seed ☐ Bulb ☐ Root ☐ Seedling ☐ Plant

Date bought _____ From where _____

Date planted _____

Where planted _____

Date germinated _____

Date (trans)planted _____

Soil amendments _____

_____

Insect damage or disease _____

_____

Date(s) harvested _____

_____

Watering frequency _____

_____

Notes _____

_____

_____

_____

_____

PLANT NAME/CULTIVAR _____

☐ Seed ☐ Bulb ☐ Root ☐ Seedling ☐ Plant

Date bought _____ From where _____

Date planted _____

Where planted _____

Date germinated _____

Date (trans)planted _____

Soil amendments _____

_____

Insect damage or disease _____

_____

Date(s) harvested _____

_____

Watering frequency _____

_____

Notes _____

_____

_____

_____

PLANT NAME/CULTIVAR _____

☐ Seed   ☐ Bulb   ☐ Root   ☐ Seedling   ☐ Plant

Date bought _____ From where _____

Date planted _____

Where planted _____

Date germinated _____

Date (trans)planted _____

Soil amendments _____

_____

Insect damage or disease _____

_____

Date(s) harvested _____

_____

Watering frequency _____

_____

Notes _____

_____

_____

_____

PLANT NAME/CULTIVAR _____

☐ Seed ☐ Bulb ☐ Root ☐ Seedling ☐ Plant

Date bought _____ From where _____

Date planted _____

Where planted _____

Date germinated _____

Date (trans)planted _____

Soil amendments _____

_____

Insect damage or disease _____

_____

Date(s) harvested _____

_____

Watering frequency _____

_____

Notes _____

_____

_____

_____

PLANT NAME/CULTIVAR _____

☐ Seed ☐ Bulb ☐ Root ☐ Seedling ☐ Plant

Date bought _____ From where _____

Date planted _____

Where planted _____

Date germinated _____

Date (trans)planted _____

Soil amendments _____

_____

Insect damage or disease _____

_____

Date(s) harvested _____

_____

Watering frequency _____

_____

Notes _____

_____

_____

_____

_____

PLANT NAME/CULTIVAR _____

☐ Seed   ☐ Bulb   ☐ Root   ☐ Seedling   ☐ Plant

Date bought _____ From where _____

Date planted _____

Where planted _____

Date germinated _____

Date (trans)planted _____

Soil amendments _____

_____

Insect damage or disease _____

_____

Date(s) harvested _____

_____

Watering frequency _____

_____

Notes _____

_____

_____

_____

_____

YEAR ONE

YEAR TWO

YEAR THREE

YEAR FOUR

YEAR FIVE

PLANT NAME/CULTIVAR _____

☐ Seed   ☐ Bulb   ☐ Root   ☐ Seedling   ☐ Plant

Date bought _____ From where _____

Date planted _____

Where planted _____

Date germinated _____

Date (trans)planted _____

Soil amendments _____

_____

Insect damage or disease _____

_____

Date(s) harvested _____

_____

Watering frequency _____

_____

Notes _____

_____

_____

_____

_____

PLANT NAME/CULTIVAR _____

☐ Seed   ☐ Bulb   ☐ Root   ☐ Seedling   ☐ Plant

Date bought _____ From where _____

Date planted _____

Where planted _____

Date germinated _____

Date (trans)planted _____

Soil amendments _____

_____

Insect damage or disease _____

_____

Date(s) harvested _____

_____

Watering frequency _____

_____

Notes _____

_____

_____

_____

_____

PLANT NAME/CULTIVAR _____

☐ Seed ☐ Bulb ☐ Root ☐ Seedling ☐ Plant

Date bought _____ From where _____

Date planted _____

Where planted _____

Date germinated _____

Date (trans)planted _____

Soil amendments _____

_____

Insect damage or disease _____

_____

Date(s) harvested _____

_____

Watering frequency _____

_____

Notes _____

_____

_____

_____

_____

PLANT NAME/CULTIVAR _____

☐ Seed   ☐ Bulb   ☐ Root   ☐ Seedling   ☐ Plant

Date bought _____ From where _____

Date planted _____

Where planted _____

Date germinated _____

Date (trans)planted _____

Soil amendments _____

_____

Insect damage or disease _____

_____

Date(s) harvested _____

_____

Watering frequency _____

_____

Notes _____

_____

_____

_____

_____

PLANT NAME/CULTIVAR _____

☐ Seed ☐ Bulb ☐ Root ☐ Seedling ☐ Plant

Date bought _____ From where _____

Date planted _____

Where planted _____

Date germinated _____

Date (trans)planted _____

Soil amendments _____

_____

Insect damage or disease _____

_____

Date(s) harvested _____

_____

Watering frequency _____

_____

Notes _____

_____

_____

_____

_____

PLANT NAME/CULTIVAR _____

☐ Seed ☐ Bulb ☐ Root ☐ Seedling ☐ Plant

Date bought _____ From where _____

Date planted _____

Where planted _____

Date germinated _____

Date (trans)planted _____

Soil amendments _____

_____

Insect damage or disease _____

_____

Date(s) harvested _____

_____

Watering frequency _____

_____

Notes _____

_____

_____

_____

YEAR ONE

YEAR TWO

YEAR THREE

YEAR FOUR

YEAR FIVE

YEAR FOUR

In nature, nothing is perfect
and everything is perfect.

-ALICE WALKER

LET'S GET THIS GARDEN STARTED

Think about what you want to grow. In the lists that follow, check whether they're annuals or perennials, sun- or shade-dwelling, and note the approximate season in which they're at their showiest. Don't limit yourself to a certain number; you will prune your list later.

List of Flower or Ornamental Plants

_____ Season _____ ☐ Annual ☐ Perennial ☐ Sun ☐ Shade

_____ Season _____ ☐ Annual ☐ Perennial ☐ Sun ☐ Shade

_____ Season _____ ☐ Annual ☐ Perennial ☐ Sun ☐ Shade

_____ Season _____ ☐ Annual ☐ Perennial ☐ Sun ☐ Shade

_____ Season _____ ☐ Annual ☐ Perennial ☐ Sun ☐ Shade

_____ Season _____ ☐ Annual ☐ Perennial ☐ Sun ☐ Shade

_____ Season _____ ☐ Annual ☐ Perennial ☐ Sun ☐ Shade

_____ Season _____ ☐ Annual ☐ Perennial ☐ Sun ☐ Shade

_____ Season _____ ☐ Annual ☐ Perennial ☐ Sun ☐ Shade

_____ Season _____ ☐ Annual ☐ Perennial ☐ Sun ☐ Shade

_____ Season _____ ☐ Annual ☐ Perennial ☐ Sun ☐ Shade

_____ Season _____ ☐ Annual ☐ Perennial ☐ Sun ☐ Shade

_____ Season _____ ☐ Annual ☐ Perennial ☐ Sun ☐ Shade

_____ Season _____ ☐ Annual ☐ Perennial ☐ Sun ☐ Shade

_____ Season _____ ☐ Annual ☐ Perennial ☐ Sun ☐ Shade

_____ Season _____ ☐ Annual ☐ Perennial ☐ Sun ☐ Shade

_____ Season _____ ☐ Annual ☐ Perennial ☐ Sun ☐ Shade

_____ Season _____ ☐ Annual ☐ Perennial ☐ Sun ☐ Shade

List of Edible Plants (Herbs, Fruits, Vegetables)

YEAR ONE

_____ Season _____ ☐ Annual ☐ Perennial ☐ Sun ☐ Shade

_____ Season _____ ☐ Annual ☐ Perennial ☐ Sun ☐ Shade

_____ Season _____ ☐ Annual ☐ Perennial ☐ Sun ☐ Shade

_____ Season _____ ☐ Annual ☐ Perennial ☐ Sun ☐ Shade

_____ Season _____ ☐ Annual ☐ Perennial ☐ Sun ☐ Shade

YEAR TWO

_____ Season _____ ☐ Annual ☐ Perennial ☐ Sun ☐ Shade

_____ Season _____ ☐ Annual ☐ Perennial ☐ Sun ☐ Shade

_____ Season _____ ☐ Annual ☐ Perennial ☐ Sun ☐ Shade

_____ Season _____ ☐ Annual ☐ Perennial ☐ Sun ☐ Shade

_____ Season _____ ☐ Annual ☐ Perennial ☐ Sun ☐ Shade

YEAR THREE

_____ Season _____ ☐ Annual ☐ Perennial ☐ Sun ☐ Shade

_____ Season _____ ☐ Annual ☐ Perennial ☐ Sun ☐ Shade

_____ Season _____ ☐ Annual ☐ Perennial ☐ Sun ☐ Shade

_____ Season _____ ☐ Annual ☐ Perennial ☐ Sun ☐ Shade

YEAR FOUR

_____ Season _____ ☐ Annual ☐ Perennial ☐ Sun ☐ Shade

_____ Season _____ ☐ Annual ☐ Perennial ☐ Sun ☐ Shade

_____ Season _____ ☐ Annual ☐ Perennial ☐ Sun ☐ Shade

_____ Season _____ ☐ Annual ☐ Perennial ☐ Sun ☐ Shade

_____ Season _____ ☐ Annual ☐ Perennial ☐ Sun ☐ Shade

YEAR FIVE

_____ Season _____ ☐ Annual ☐ Perennial ☐ Sun ☐ Shade

_____ Season _____ ☐ Annual ☐ Perennial ☐ Sun ☐ Shade

_____ Season _____ ☐ Annual ☐ Perennial ☐ Sun ☐ Shade

MAKE A LIST, CHECK IT TWICE

Review your lists on the previous pages and write down your plant choices, starting with your top picks. Note which you'll sow directly in your garden, which you'll start indoors or buy as seedlings, and which you'll wait to buy as larger plants. Jot down approximate date(s) that you will need to direct sow or start seeds as well as what you'll need for each of them. Complete an inventory of what you saved from last year and place a checkmark next to any seeds or bulbs you can still use.

_____ plant date _____
☐ direct sow ☐ start as seeds ☐ buy seedlings ☐ buy plants

_____ plant date _____
☐ direct sow ☐ start as seeds ☐ buy seedlings ☐ buy plants

_____ plant date _____
☐ direct sow ☐ start as seeds ☐ buy seedlings ☐ buy plants

_____ plant date _____
☐ direct sow ☐ start as seeds ☐ buy seedlings ☐ buy plants

_____ plant date _____
☐ direct sow ☐ start as seeds ☐ buy seedlings ☐ buy plants

_____ plant date _____
☐ direct sow ☐ start as seeds ☐ buy seedlings ☐ buy plants

_____ plant date _____
☐ direct sow ☐ start as seeds ☐ buy seedlings ☐ buy plants

_____ plant date _____
☐ direct sow ☐ start as seeds ☐ buy seedlings ☐ buy plants

_____ plant date _____
☐ direct sow ☐ start as seeds ☐ buy seedlings ☐ buy plants

_____ plant date _____
☐ direct sow ☐ start as seeds ☐ buy seedlings ☐ buy plants

_____ plant date _____
☐ direct sow ☐ start as seeds ☐ buy seedlings ☐ buy plants

_____ plant date _____
☐ direct sow ☐ start as seeds ☐ buy seedlings ☐ buy plants

_____ plant date _____
☐ direct sow ☐ start as seeds ☐ buy seedlings ☐ buy plants

_____ plant date _____
☐ direct sow ☐ start as seeds ☐ buy seedlings ☐ buy plants

_____ plant date _____
☐ direct sow ☐ start as seeds ☐ buy seedlings ☐ buy plants

_____ plant date _____
☐ direct sow ☐ start as seeds ☐ buy seedlings ☐ buy plants

_____ plant date _____
☐ direct sow ☐ start as seeds ☐ buy seedlings ☐ buy plants

_____ plant date _____
☐ direct sow ☐ start as seeds ☐ buy seedlings ☐ buy plants

_____ plant date _____
☐ direct sow ☐ start as seeds ☐ buy seedlings ☐ buy plants

_____ plant date _____
☐ direct sow ☐ start as seeds ☐ buy seedlings ☐ buy plants

_____ plant date _____
☐ direct sow ☐ start as seeds ☐ buy seedlings ☐ buy plants

_____ plant date _____
☐ direct sow ☐ start as seeds ☐ buy seedlings ☐ buy plants

_____ plant date _____
☐ direct sow ☐ start as seeds ☐ buy seedlings ☐ buy plants

_____ plant date _____
☐ direct sow ☐ start as seeds ☐ buy seedlings ☐ buy plants

WHAT GOES WHERE

Map out your garden(s) here. Start with the plants at the top of your list from page 109 to make sure you have enough room for them. You might find that you have to narrow your lists even more—or that you have room to add others.

SAVE THOSE TAGS

Every plant you buy comes with a little label or tag with care instructions that includes sun and water preference. Use these pages to tape them in so you always have them. If the tags are dirty, or you'd rather not paste them here, then jot down some care instructions (and use the tags to label your plants).

YEAR ONE

YEAR TWO

YEAR THREE

YEAR FOUR

YEAR FIVE

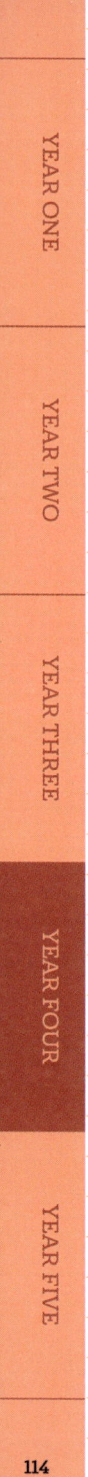

PLANTS LOG

Keep a running list of your plants in these pages. Make notes about any troubles or successes, whether you'll plant something again, or anything else you might keep or change up.

PLANT NAME/CULTIVAR _____

☐ Seed ☐ Bulb ☐ Root ☐ Seedling ☐ Plant

Date bought _____ From where _____

Date planted _____

Where planted _____

Date germinated _____

Date (trans)planted _____

Soil amendments _____

Insect damage or disease _____

_____

Date(s) harvested _____

_____

Watering frequency _____

_____

Notes _____

_____

PLANT NAME/CULTIVAR _____

☐ Seed ☐ Bulb ☐ Root ☐ Seedling ☐ Plant

Date bought _____ From where _____

Date planted _____

Where planted _____

Date germinated _____

Date (trans)planted _____

Soil amendments _____

_____

Insect damage or disease _____

_____

Date(s) harvested _____

_____

Watering frequency _____

_____

Notes _____

_____

_____

_____

_____

PLANT NAME/CULTIVAR _____

☐ Seed   ☐ Bulb   ☐ Root   ☐ Seedling   ☐ Plant

Date bought _____ From where _____

Date planted _____

Where planted _____

Date germinated _____

Date (trans)planted _____

Soil amendments _____

_____

Insect damage or disease _____

_____

Date(s) harvested _____

_____

Watering frequency _____

_____

Notes _____

_____

_____

_____

PLANT NAME/CULTIVAR _____

☐ Seed ☐ Bulb ☐ Root ☐ Seedling ☐ Plant

Date bought _____ From where _____

Date planted _____

Where planted _____

Date germinated _____

Date (trans)planted _____

Soil amendments _____

_____

Insect damage or disease _____

_____

Date(s) harvested _____

_____

Watering frequency _____

_____

Notes _____

_____

_____

_____

_____

PLANT NAME/CULTIVAR _____

☐ Seed   ☐ Bulb   ☐ Root   ☐ Seedling   ☐ Plant

Date bought _____ From where _____

Date planted _____

Where planted _____

Date germinated _____

Date (trans)planted _____

Soil amendments _____

_____

Insect damage or disease _____

_____

Date(s) harvested _____

_____

Watering frequency _____

_____

Notes _____

_____

_____

_____

_____

PLANT NAME/CULTIVAR _____

☐ Seed ☐ Bulb ☐ Root ☐ Seedling ☐ Plant

Date bought _____ From where _____

Date planted _____

Where planted _____

Date germinated _____

Date (trans)planted _____

Soil amendments _____

_____

Insect damage or disease _____

_____

Date(s) harvested _____

_____

Watering frequency _____

_____

Notes _____

_____

_____

_____

_____

PLANT NAME/CULTIVAR _____

☐ Seed ☐ Bulb ☐ Root ☐ Seedling ☐ Plant

Date bought _____ From where _____

Date planted _____

Where planted _____

Date germinated _____

Date (trans)planted _____

Soil amendments _____

_____

Insect damage or disease _____

_____

Date(s) harvested _____

_____

Watering frequency _____

_____

Notes _____

_____

_____

_____

_____

PLANT NAME/CULTIVAR _____

☐ Seed   ☐ Bulb   ☐ Root   ☐ Seedling   ☐ Plant

Date bought _____ From where _____

Date planted _____

Where planted _____

Date germinated _____

Date (trans)planted _____

Soil amendments _____

_____

Insect damage or disease _____

_____

Date(s) harvested _____

_____

Watering frequency _____

_____

Notes _____

_____

_____

_____

_____

PLANT NAME/CULTIVAR _____

☐ Seed   ☐ Bulb   ☐ Root   ☐ Seedling   ☐ Plant

Date bought _____ From where _____

Date planted _____

Where planted _____

Date germinated _____

Date (trans)planted _____

Soil amendments _____
_____

Insect damage or disease _____
_____

Date(s) harvested _____
_____

Watering frequency _____
_____

Notes _____
_____
_____
_____
_____

PLANT NAME/CULTIVAR _____

☐ Seed ☐ Bulb ☐ Root ☐ Seedling ☐ Plant

Date bought _____ From where _____

Date planted _____

Where planted _____

Date germinated _____

Date (trans)planted _____

Soil amendments _____
_____

Insect damage or disease _____
_____

Date(s) harvested _____
_____

Watering frequency _____
_____

Notes _____
_____
_____
_____
_____

PLANT NAME/CULTIVAR _____

☐ Seed   ☐ Bulb   ☐ Root   ☐ Seedling   ☐ Plant

Date bought _____ From where _____

Date planted _____

Where planted _____

Date germinated _____

Date (trans)planted _____

Soil amendments _____

_____

Insect damage or disease _____

_____

Date(s) harvested _____

_____

Watering frequency _____

_____

Notes _____

_____

_____

_____

PLANT NAME/CULTIVAR _____

☐ Seed ☐ Bulb ☐ Root ☐ Seedling ☐ Plant

Date bought _____ From where _____

Date planted _____

Where planted _____

Date germinated _____

Date (trans)planted _____

Soil amendments _____

_____

Insect damage or disease _____

_____

Date(s) harvested _____

_____

Watering frequency _____

_____

Notes _____

_____

_____

_____

_____

PLANT NAME/CULTIVAR _____

☐ Seed   ☐ Bulb   ☐ Root   ☐ Seedling   ☐ Plant

Date bought _____ From where _____

Date planted _____

Where planted _____

Date germinated _____

Date (trans)planted _____

Soil amendments _____

_____

Insect damage or disease _____

_____

Date(s) harvested _____

_____

Watering frequency _____

_____

Notes _____

_____

_____

_____

_____

PLANT NAME/CULTIVAR _____

☐ Seed   ☐ Bulb   ☐ Root   ☐ Seedling   ☐ Plant

Date bought _____ From where _____

Date planted _____

Where planted _____

Date germinated _____

Date (trans)planted _____

Soil amendments _____

_____

Insect damage or disease _____

_____

Date(s) harvested _____

_____

Watering frequency _____

_____

Notes _____

_____

_____

_____

_____

PLANT NAME/CULTIVAR _____

☐ Seed ☐ Bulb ☐ Root ☐ Seedling ☐ Plant

Date bought _____ From where _____

Date planted _____

Where planted _____

Date germinated _____

Date (trans)planted _____

Soil amendments _____

_____

Insect damage or disease _____

_____

Date(s) harvested _____

_____

Watering frequency _____

_____

Notes _____

_____

_____

_____

_____

PLANT NAME/CULTIVAR _____

☐ Seed ☐ Bulb ☐ Root ☐ Seedling ☐ Plant

Date bought _____ From where _____

Date planted _____

Where planted _____

Date germinated _____

Date (trans)planted _____

Soil amendments _____

_____

Insect damage or disease _____

_____

Date(s) harvested _____

_____

Watering frequency _____

_____

Notes _____

_____

_____

_____

_____

PLANT NAME/CULTIVAR _____

☐ Seed   ☐ Bulb   ☐ Root   ☐ Seedling   ☐ Plant

Date bought _____ From where _____

Date planted _____

Where planted _____

Date germinated _____

Date (trans)planted _____

Soil amendments _____

_____

Insect damage or disease _____

_____

Date(s) harvested _____

_____

Watering frequency _____

_____

Notes _____

_____

_____

_____

_____

PLANT NAME/CULTIVAR _____

☐ Seed   ☐ Bulb   ☐ Root   ☐ Seedling   ☐ Plant

Date bought _____ From where _____

Date planted _____

Where planted _____

Date germinated _____

Date (trans)planted _____

Soil amendments _____

_____

Insect damage or disease _____

_____

Date(s) harvested _____

_____

Watering frequency _____

_____

Notes _____

_____

_____

_____

_____

YEAR FIVE

Despite the gardener's best intentions,
Nature will improvise.

-MICHAEL P. GAROFALO

LET'S GET THIS GARDEN STARTED

Think about what you want to grow. In the lists that follow, check whether they're annuals or perennials, sun- or shade-dwelling, and note the approximate season in which they're at their showiest. Don't limit yourself to a certain number; you will prune your list later.

List of Flower or Ornamental Plants

_____ Season _____ ☐ Annual ☐ Perennial ☐ Sun ☐ Shade

_____ Season _____ ☐ Annual ☐ Perennial ☐ Sun ☐ Shade

_____ Season _____ ☐ Annual ☐ Perennial ☐ Sun ☐ Shade

_____ Season _____ ☐ Annual ☐ Perennial ☐ Sun ☐ Shade

_____ Season _____ ☐ Annual ☐ Perennial ☐ Sun ☐ Shade

_____ Season _____ ☐ Annual ☐ Perennial ☐ Sun ☐ Shade

_____ Season _____ ☐ Annual ☐ Perennial ☐ Sun ☐ Shade

_____ Season _____ ☐ Annual ☐ Perennial ☐ Sun ☐ Shade

_____ Season _____ ☐ Annual ☐ Perennial ☐ Sun ☐ Shade

_____ Season _____ ☐ Annual ☐ Perennial ☐ Sun ☐ Shade

_____ Season _____ ☐ Annual ☐ Perennial ☐ Sun ☐ Shade

_____ Season _____ ☐ Annual ☐ Perennial ☐ Sun ☐ Shade

_____ Season _____ ☐ Annual ☐ Perennial ☐ Sun ☐ Shade

_____ Season _____ ☐ Annual ☐ Perennial ☐ Sun ☐ Shade

_____ Season _____ ☐ Annual ☐ Perennial ☐ Sun ☐ Shade

_____ Season _____ ☐ Annual ☐ Perennial ☐ Sun ☐ Shade

_____ Season _____ ☐ Annual ☐ Perennial ☐ Sun ☐ Shade

_____ Season _____ ☐ Annual ☐ Perennial ☐ Sun ☐ Shade

_____ Season _____ ☐ Annual ☐ Perennial ☐ Sun ☐ Shade

List of Edible Plants (Herbs, Fruits, Vegetables)

_____ Season _____ ☐ Annual ☐ Perennial ☐ Sun ☐ Shade

_____ Season _____ ☐ Annual ☐ Perennial ☐ Sun ☐ Shade

_____ Season _____ ☐ Annual ☐ Perennial ☐ Sun ☐ Shade

_____ Season _____ ☐ Annual ☐ Perennial ☐ Sun ☐ Shade

_____ Season _____ ☐ Annual ☐ Perennial ☐ Sun ☐ Shade

_____ Season _____ ☐ Annual ☐ Perennial ☐ Sun ☐ Shade

_____ Season _____ ☐ Annual ☐ Perennial ☐ Sun ☐ Shade

_____ Season _____ ☐ Annual ☐ Perennial ☐ Sun ☐ Shade

_____ Season _____ ☐ Annual ☐ Perennial ☐ Sun ☐ Shade

_____ Season _____ ☐ Annual ☐ Perennial ☐ Sun ☐ Shade

_____ Season _____ ☐ Annual ☐ Perennial ☐ Sun ☐ Shade

_____ Season _____ ☐ Annual ☐ Perennial ☐ Sun ☐ Shade

_____ Season _____ ☐ Annual ☐ Perennial ☐ Sun ☐ Shade

_____ Season _____ ☐ Annual ☐ Perennial ☐ Sun ☐ Shade

_____ Season _____ ☐ Annual ☐ Perennial ☐ Sun ☐ Shade

_____ Season _____ ☐ Annual ☐ Perennial ☐ Sun ☐ Shade

_____ Season _____ ☐ Annual ☐ Perennial ☐ Sun ☐ Shade

_____ Season _____ ☐ Annual ☐ Perennial ☐ Sun ☐ Shade

_____ Season _____ ☐ Annual ☐ Perennial ☐ Sun ☐ Shade

_____ Season _____ ☐ Annual ☐ Perennial ☐ Sun ☐ Shade

_____ Season _____ ☐ Annual ☐ Perennial ☐ Sun ☐ Shade

_____ Season _____ ☐ Annual ☐ Perennial ☐ Sun ☐ Shade

_____ Season _____ ☐ Annual ☐ Perennial ☐ Sun ☐ Shade

_____ Season _____ ☐ Annual ☐ Perennial ☐ Sun ☐ Shade

MAKE A LIST, CHECK IT TWICE

Review your lists on the previous pages and write down your plant choices, starting with your top picks. Note which you'll sow directly in your garden, which you'll start indoors or buy as seedlings, and which you'll wait to buy as larger plants. Jot down approximate date(s) that you will need to direct sow or start seeds as well as what you'll need for each of them. Complete an inventory of what you saved from last year and place a checkmark next to any seeds or bulbs you can still use.

_____ plant date _____
☐ direct sow ☐ start as seeds ☐ buy seedlings ☐ buy plants

_____ plant date _____
☐ direct sow ☐ start as seeds ☐ buy seedlings ☐ buy plants

_____ plant date _____
☐ direct sow ☐ start as seeds ☐ buy seedlings ☐ buy plants

_____ plant date _____
☐ direct sow ☐ start as seeds ☐ buy seedlings ☐ buy plants

_____ plant date _____
☐ direct sow ☐ start as seeds ☐ buy seedlings ☐ buy plants

_____ plant date _____
☐ direct sow ☐ start as seeds ☐ buy seedlings ☐ buy plants

_____ plant date _____
☐ direct sow ☐ start as seeds ☐ buy seedlings ☐ buy plants

_____ plant date _____
☐ direct sow ☐ start as seeds ☐ buy seedlings ☐ buy plants

_____ plant date _____
☐ direct sow ☐ start as seeds ☐ buy seedlings ☐ buy plants

_____ plant date _____
☐ direct sow ☐ start as seeds ☐ buy seedlings ☐ buy plants

_____ plant date _____

☐ direct sow ☐ start as seeds ☐ buy seedlings ☐ buy plants

_____ plant date _____

☐ direct sow ☐ start as seeds ☐ buy seedlings ☐ buy plants

_____ plant date _____

☐ direct sow ☐ start as seeds ☐ buy seedlings ☐ buy plants

_____ plant date _____

☐ direct sow ☐ start as seeds ☐ buy seedlings ☐ buy plants

_____ plant date _____

☐ direct sow ☐ start as seeds ☐ buy seedlings ☐ buy plants

_____ plant date _____

☐ direct sow ☐ start as seeds ☐ buy seedlings ☐ buy plants

_____ plant date _____

☐ direct sow ☐ start as seeds ☐ buy seedlings ☐ buy plants

_____ plant date _____

☐ direct sow ☐ start as seeds ☐ buy seedlings ☐ buy plants

_____ plant date _____

☐ direct sow ☐ start as seeds ☐ buy seedlings ☐ buy plants

_____ plant date _____

☐ direct sow ☐ start as seeds ☐ buy seedlings ☐ buy plants

_____ plant date _____

☐ direct sow ☐ start as seeds ☐ buy seedlings ☐ buy plants

_____ plant date _____

☐ direct sow ☐ start as seeds ☐ buy seedlings ☐ buy plants

_____ plant date _____

☐ direct sow ☐ start as seeds ☐ buy seedlings ☐ buy plants

WHAT GOES WHERE

Map out your garden(s) here. Start with the plants at the top of your list from page 136 to make sure you have enough room for them. You might find that you have to narrow your lists even more—or that you have room to add others.

SAVE THOSE TAGS

Every plant you buy comes with a little label or tag with care instructions that includes sun and water preference. Use these pages to tape them in so you always have them. If the tags are dirty, or you'd rather not paste them here, then jot down some care instructions (and use the tags to label your plants).

PLANTS LOG

Keep a running list of your plants in these pages. Make notes about any troubles or successes, whether you'll plant something again, or anything else you might keep or change up.

PLANT NAME/CULTIVAR _____

☐ Seed ☐ Bulb ☐ Root ☐ Seedling ☐ Plant

Date bought _____ From where _____

Date planted _____

Where planted _____

Date germinated _____

Date (trans)planted _____

Soil amendments _____

Insect damage or disease _____

_____

Date(s) harvested _____

_____

Watering frequency _____

_____

Notes _____

_____

PLANT NAME/CULTIVAR _____

☐ Seed ☐ Bulb ☐ Root ☐ Seedling ☐ Plant

Date bought _____ From where _____

Date planted _____

Where planted _____

Date germinated _____

Date (trans)planted _____

Soil amendments _____

_____

Insect damage or disease _____

_____

Date(s) harvested _____

_____

Watering frequency _____

_____

Notes _____

_____

_____

_____

PLANT NAME/CULTIVAR _____

☐ Seed ☐ Bulb ☐ Root ☐ Seedling ☐ Plant

Date bought _____ From where _____

Date planted _____

Where planted _____

Date germinated _____

Date (trans)planted _____

Soil amendments _____

_____

Insect damage or disease _____

_____

Date(s) harvested _____

_____

Watering frequency _____

_____

Notes _____

_____

_____

_____

_____

PLANT NAME/CULTIVAR _____

☐ Seed   ☐ Bulb   ☐ Root   ☐ Seedling   ☐ Plant

Date bought _____ From where _____

Date planted _____

Where planted _____

Date germinated _____

Date (trans)planted _____

Soil amendments _____

_____

Insect damage or disease _____

_____

Date(s) harvested _____

_____

Watering frequency _____

_____

Notes _____

_____

_____

_____

_____

PLANT NAME/CULTIVAR _____

☐ Seed   ☐ Bulb   ☐ Root   ☐ Seedling   ☐ Plant

Date bought _____ From where _____

Date planted _____

Where planted _____

Date germinated _____

Date (trans)planted _____

Soil amendments _____

_____

Insect damage or disease _____

_____

Date(s) harvested _____

_____

Watering frequency _____

_____

Notes _____

_____

_____

_____

_____

PLANT NAME/CULTIVAR _____

☐ Seed ☐ Bulb ☐ Root ☐ Seedling ☐ Plant

Date bought _____ From where _____

Date planted _____

Where planted _____

Date germinated _____

Date (trans)planted _____

Soil amendments _____

_____

Insect damage or disease _____

_____

Date(s) harvested _____

_____

Watering frequency _____

_____

Notes _____

_____

_____

_____

_____

PLANT NAME/CULTIVAR _____

☐ Seed   ☐ Bulb   ☐ Root   ☐ Seedling   ☐ Plant

Date bought _____ From where _____

Date planted _____

Where planted _____

Date germinated _____

Date (trans)planted _____

Soil amendments _____

_____

Insect damage or disease _____

_____

Date(s) harvested _____

_____

Watering frequency _____

_____

Notes _____

_____

_____

_____

_____

PLANT NAME/CULTIVAR _____

☐ Seed   ☐ Bulb   ☐ Root   ☐ Seedling   ☐ Plant

Date bought _____ From where _____

Date planted _____

Where planted _____

Date germinated _____

Date (trans)planted _____

Soil amendments _____

_____

Insect damage or disease _____

_____

Date(s) harvested _____

_____

Watering frequency _____

_____

Notes _____

_____

_____

_____

PLANT NAME/CULTIVAR _____

☐ Seed   ☐ Bulb   ☐ Root   ☐ Seedling   ☐ Plant

Date bought _____ From where _____

Date planted _____

Where planted _____

Date germinated _____

Date (trans)planted _____

Soil amendments _____

_____

Insect damage or disease _____

_____

Date(s) harvested _____

_____

Watering frequency _____

_____

Notes _____

_____

_____

_____

_____

PLANT NAME/CULTIVAR _____

☐ Seed   ☐ Bulb   ☐ Root   ☐ Seedling   ☐ Plant

Date bought _____ From where _____

Date planted _____

Where planted _____

Date germinated _____

Date (trans)planted _____

Soil amendments _____

_____

Insect damage or disease _____

_____

Date(s) harvested _____

_____

Watering frequency _____

_____

Notes _____

_____

_____

_____

_____

PLANT NAME/CULTIVAR _____

☐ Seed   ☐ Bulb   ☐ Root   ☐ Seedling   ☐ Plant

Date bought _____ From where _____

Date planted _____

Where planted _____

Date germinated _____

Date (trans)planted _____

Soil amendments _____

_____

Insect damage or disease _____

_____

Date(s) harvested _____

_____

Watering frequency _____

_____

Notes _____

_____

_____

_____

_____

PLANT NAME/CULTIVAR _____

☐ Seed   ☐ Bulb   ☐ Root   ☐ Seedling   ☐ Plant

Date bought _____ From where _____

Date planted _____

Where planted _____

Date germinated _____

Date (trans)planted _____

Soil amendments _____

_____

Insect damage or disease _____

_____

Date(s) harvested _____

_____

Watering frequency _____

_____

Notes _____

_____

_____

_____

_____

PLANT NAME/CULTIVAR _____

☐ Seed ☐ Bulb ☐ Root ☐ Seedling ☐ Plant

Date bought _____ From where _____

Date planted _____

Where planted _____

Date germinated _____

Date (trans)planted _____

Soil amendments _____

_____

Insect damage or disease _____

_____

Date(s) harvested _____

_____

Watering frequency _____

_____

Notes _____

_____

_____

_____

_____

PLANT NAME/CULTIVAR _____

☐ Seed   ☐ Bulb   ☐ Root   ☐ Seedling   ☐ Plant

Date bought _____ From where _____

Date planted _____

Where planted _____

Date germinated _____

Date (trans)planted _____

Soil amendments _____

_____

Insect damage or disease _____

_____

Date(s) harvested _____

_____

Watering frequency _____

_____

Notes _____

_____

_____

_____

_____

PLANT NAME/CULTIVAR _____

☐ Seed   ☐ Bulb   ☐ Root   ☐ Seedling   ☐ Plant

Date bought _____ From where _____

Date planted _____

Where planted _____

Date germinated _____

Date (trans)planted _____

Soil amendments _____
_____

Insect damage or disease _____
_____

Date(s) harvested _____
_____

Watering frequency _____
_____

Notes _____
_____
_____
_____
_____

PLANT NAME/CULTIVAR _____

☐ Seed ☐ Bulb ☐ Root ☐ Seedling ☐ Plant

Date bought _____ From where _____

Date planted _____

Where planted _____

Date germinated _____

Date (trans)planted _____

Soil amendments _____

_____

Insect damage or disease _____

_____

Date(s) harvested _____

_____

Watering frequency _____

_____

Notes _____

_____

_____

_____

_____

YEAR ONE

YEAR TWO

YEAR THREE

YEAR FOUR

YEAR FIVE

PLANT NAME/CULTIVAR

☐ Seed   ☐ Bulb   ☐ Root   ☐ Seedling   ☐ Plant

Date bought _____ From where _____

Date planted _____

Where planted _____

Date germinated _____

Date (trans)planted _____

Soil amendments _____

_____

Insect damage or disease _____

_____

Date(s) harvested _____

_____

Watering frequency _____

_____

Notes _____

_____

_____

_____

_____

PLANT NAME/CULTIVAR _____

☐ Seed ☐ Bulb ☐ Root ☐ Seedling ☐ Plant

Date bought _____ From where _____

Date planted _____

Where planted _____

Date germinated _____

Date (trans)planted _____

Soil amendments _____

_____

Insect damage or disease _____

_____

Date(s) harvested _____

_____

Watering frequency _____

_____

Notes _____

_____

_____

_____

_____

Brimming with creative inspiration, how-to projects, and useful information to enrich your everyday life, quarto.com is a favorite destination for those pursuing their interests and passions.

This edition published in 2023 by Chartwell Books, an imprint of The Quarto Group
142 West 36th Street, 4th Floor
New York, NY 10018 USA
T (212) 779-4972 F (212) 779-6058
www.Quarto.com

10 9 8 7 6 5 4 3 2 1

Chartwell titles are also available at discount for retail, wholesale, promotional, and bulk purchase. For details, contact the Special Sales Manager by email at specialsales@quarto.com or by mail at The Quarto Group, Attn: Special Sales Manager, 100 Cummings Center Suite 265D, Beverly, MA 01915, USA.

ISBN: 978-0-7858-4201-9

Publisher: Wendy Friedman
Senior Managing Editor: Meredith Mennitt
Senior Design Manager: Michael Caputo
Editor: Jennifer Kushnier
Designer: Kate Sinclair

All stock photos & design elements ©Shutterstock

Printed in China

References: The Big Book of Gardening Secrets (Storey Communications, Inc., 1998) and Rodale's Garden Answers (Rodale Press, Inc., 1995).